GOLF COURSES
YOU'LL NEVER PLAY

GOLF COURSES
YOU'LL NEVER PLAY

James Becker & Andrew Mayer
Illustrations by Robert Greisen

MACMILLAN • USA

MACMILLAN
A Simon & Schuster Macmillan Company
15 Columbus Circle
New York, NY 10023

Macmillan is a registered trademark of Macmillan, Inc.
Book and cover design: Suzanne Brooker
Illustrations: Bob Greisen

Library of Congress Cataloging-in-Publication Data

Becker, James.
    Golf courses you'll never play/by James Becker
& Andrew Mayer.
        p.   cm.
    ISBN 0-02-508210-8
    1. Golf—Humor.   2. Golf courses.   3. Imaginary places.
I. Mayer, Andrew, 1954–   II. Title.
GV967.B445   1995
796.35206'8'0207—dc20   94-38537

10 9 8 7 6 5 4 3 2 1

FROM THE TAJ MAHAL MAUSOLEUM, GOLF & COUNTRY CLUB
*Right: At 344 yards, the signature 18th plays almost entirely over
water. Here is a hole that challenges even the likes of John Daly.*

Photo: Louis H. Jawitz/The Image Bank

FROM THE RUINS, STONEHENGE GOLF & COUNTRY CLUB.
*Cover: A player tees off from the elevated black tees on the
par-4 10th hole. Maintaining your footing is an absolute
necessity when teeing off from atop one of these big rocks.*

Photo: Patrick Eden/The Image Bank

18th
Hole

Par 3
344 Yards

$\mathcal{T}able\ of\ \mathcal{C}ontents$

24

THE TAJ MAHAL
MAUSOLEUM, GOLF
& COUNTRY CLUB

Agra, India

36

THE RUINS, STONEHENGE
GOLF & COUNTRY CLUB

Salisbury Plain, England

28

THE NEW YORK STOCK
EXCHANGE & COUNTRY CLUB

Wall Street
New York City, New York

40

THE VATICAN CITY GOLF
& COUNTRY CLUB

Vatican City
Rome, Italy

32

THE GREAT PYRAMIDS

Giza, Egypt

44

THE PRESIDENTIAL COURSE

The White House
Washington, D.C.
United States

Her Majesty's Golf & Cricket Club
Buckingham Palace
London, England

HER MAJESTY'S GOLF & CRICKET CLUB, or simply "Her Majesty's"—as it is referred to by those in the know—dates back to the sixteenth century. This fine old course was built on Church land that was seized by Henry VIII. Because the clergy had little or no interest in golf, it fell to the Crown to develop this land to its full potential. Throughout his reign, Henry was an avid linkster, although he never got his handicap below 20 and routinely beheaded his caddies for minor infractions.

Her Majesty's is one of the best-maintained courses in the world. A grounds crew numbering in the thousands makes sure that no blade of grass or grain of sand is out of place.

Photo:
Hans Wolf/The Image Bank

Situated on 800 acres of splendid royal parkland, Her Majesty's is a grand, mature course. Over 7,000 groundskeepers, or Beefeaters as they are called, maintain this course in their impeccable traditional red suits and furry chapeaux. Armed with bayoneted rifles, these Beefeaters have also been known to quickly dispatch golfers who advance too slowly and hold up play behind them. If you're planning to play Her Majesty's, be forewarned: keep up the pace!

The signature 7th hole is a dog-leg left, 585-yard par 5—or so we are told. Shrouded in a dense London fog day in and day out, the actual fairway and flag have rarely been sighted. A par here is no easy task. As you tee off at the 7th, pay close attention to the tee boxes. Here and elsewhere at Her Majesty's, the purple tee boxes are reserved for royalty only. Violations of this rule are not looked upon kindly!

The back nine begins with a lovely, straight-ahead, 453-yard par 4. You'll tee off at the Victoria Memorial with the stunning Buckingham Palace clubhouse within view. At 100 yards from the pin, you'll find Clarence House on your right. There you can call ahead for tea and crumpets, which will be brought out to your cart. As you putt out for par at Trafalgar Square and then prepare to tee off high atop Nelson's Column for the 11th, you'll feel as if you've made a little history of your own.

God save the Queen!

Designed by Henry VIII; 7,945 yards, par 72. Course plays slow; allow eight to nine hours for a full round. The 600-room Buckingham Palace clubhouse can accommodate private functions of up to 10,000. Bowlers required for men; any type of odd pastel hat for women is acceptable. Call the Queen Mother for tee times.

The 600-room Buckingham Palace clubhouse can easily accommodate even the largest of social gatherings.

Photo: Derek P. Redfearn/The Image Bank

The Forbidden City Country Club
(Formerly The People's Golf & Country Club)

Beijing, China

The FORBIDDEN CITY is a course in transition. For more than 500 years this 250-acre complex of temples and palaces was little more than the residence of the emperor and the center from which China was ruled. Hard as it is to believe, for many years there was no golf course here whatsoever! It wasn't until the Communist revolution of 1949 that the People's Golf & Country Club came into existence.

Mao, of course, was an avid golfer and believed that everyone should play the game. During Mao's rule, over a billion comrades a week came to hook and slice their shots at The Forbidden City, then known as People's. Getting a tee time was next to impossible, and the greens were under constant repair. It was not until China opened her gates to the public in the 1970s that the Forbidden City finally reached its true potential as a world-class golf resort destination.

The City resembles a giant miniature golf course. What exactly the course's original architects had in mind remains unclear. Today, though, the City stands alone in course architecture for its bold and truly revolutionary design.

Reflecting pools and the Gate of Supreme Harmony border the lovely 7th hole at the Forbidden City Country Club.

Photo:
Tom Owen Edmunds/The Image Bank

The 3rd hole is a dog-leg left, 220-yard par 5. Don't be fooled by the short yardage and think a birdie is at hand; the ample green for the 3rd is situated smack-dab in the middle of the Rain Flower Pavilion! Your approach shot must be hit just so to gain entrance

The main gate to the Forbidden City Golf & Country Club. The translation reads: "Welcome Golfers. May you find Par. Absolutely no spikes in the Clubhouse!"

Photo: Guido Alberto Rossi/The Image Bank

through the archway, lest you find yourself on the pavilion's ceramic roof. Once inside, it takes a gentle touch to guide your ball into the mouth of the golden dragon for par.

For the 14th you'll tee off from atop the Meridian Gate. From here you can survey the entire course, along with the finest assemblage of Ming architecture to be found anywhere in China. This dog-leg left, dog-leg right, dog-leg left, dog-leg right, 585-yard, par-5 hole takes you back and forth over the perimeter

moat too many times to count. The difficulty of the water hazard is further compounded by the fact that there is no apparent way to walk or drive your cart across the moat.

Perhaps the most stunning hole at the Forbidden City Golf & Country Club is the par-4, 385-yard 18th. This blissful hole plays east to west and is lined with lovely old palms. As with so

many holes at the City, once again you'll find yourself putting out in an ancient pavilion. Here in the Hall of Supreme Harmony, according to ancient Chinese texts, "Earth and sky meet, the four seasons merge, wind and rain are gathered in, and yin and yang are in harmony." If you can't putt out in two here, you can't putt out in two anywhere!

Designed by the People following the Communist revolution; 2,345 yards, par 72. A resident acupuncturist is available to correct your hook, slice, or any other problems you may be experiencing with your game. Call five years in advance for tee times.

Crisscrossing fairways are but one of the unique architectural features of this course. The kiosk in the foreground houses an ambitious entrepreneur who will wash your golf ball by hand in the traditional manner.

Photo: Tom Owen Edmunds/The Image Bank

The Imperial Palace
(Host of the Zen Masters)

Tokyo, Japan

NATURE HAS ALWAYS OCCUPIED a central position in the culture of Japan, and nowhere is this more evident than in the stunning design of the Imperial Palace. Pine trees, willow groves, and a variety of grasses provide the framework from which the Palace course is crafted. Mossy boulders are strategically placed on many of the fairways, and unexpected ponds appear as if out of nowhere. And then, of course, there are the bunkers.

The Palace boasts over two hundred bunkers in all, each maintained by its own grounds-keeper working with his personal staff of ten. Designed with brilliantly white sand, each bunker is given its own unique geometric pattern, which bespeaks the bunker's inner soul.

As you contemplate yet another impending double bogey from one of these lovely traps, it is here that you may unearth a moment of much-needed serenity. (While playing the Palace, please remember not to rake the traps after you play. Only members of the Palace grounds crew are accorded this privilege, and many have trained a lifetime to be permitted the honor of "guiding the rake.")

The dog-leg left 7th provides a lovely view of the Imperial Palace & Clubhouse. You'll need a straight drive to steer clear of the Palace moat, which borders the fairway down the left side. At the 100-yard marker you'll find a nondescript hut off to the right. This Izakaya, or watering hole, serves a variety of sushi along with sake—a welcome sight to the weary golfer!

Don't expect to see a bunker raked like this anywhere in the world but at the Palace!

Photo: Michael Melford/The Image Bank

Many of the lovely moats surrounding the Palace were partially or completely drained to reclaim needed land for the East Garden Course.

Photo: Holton Collection/Superstock

The signature hole at the Palace is the par-5, 595-yard 15th. Named after a Shogun warrior who committed hara-kiri after his three-putt double bogey, the Tokugawa is not quite as difficult a hole as this bit of history might suggest. Even so, with a total of twenty-eight sand traps, there is ample opportunity here to test your bunker game. Play your approach shot to the front of the green to avoid the bordering willows, which obscure much of the green and shelter the ever-present Zen monks who sit beneath them in prayer.

Nestled in the midst of polluted and congested modern-day Tokyo, the Palace provides true sanctuary—for golfers of all abilities.

Old Course designed in the fifteenth century by Ota Dokan, a minor feudal lord. Palace Course is 6,715 yards, par 72. East Garden Course is 6,445 yards, par 71. The new Palace Course and East Garden both designed by Tom Fazio. Call the emperor's personal secretary for tee times. (Before heading out, don't forget to grab one of the delightful little scorekeeping abacuses sold at the pro shop!)

A golfer carefully makes his way to the green at the 17th on a serene spring morning at the Imperial Palace course.

Photo: Steve Vidler/Superstock

The Tower
Pisa, Italy

A RELENTLESS WIND BLOWS HEAD-ON as you survey the course below you—way below you. You dig your cleats into the 800-Year-old stonework and position yourself for the 18th-hole flag, which lies 493 yards straight ahead. Just to the east, a gondolier slowly moves a foursome out to the floating 17th green. As you prepare to address the ball from the highly elevated championship tees, you can't quite shake the feeling that things are a bit off-center. Nowhere else will you find a finishing test more demanding than the world-famous 18th at the Tower.

Called the *Piazza del Miracoli*, or place of wonders, the 18th hole is aptly named: you will surely wonder what has happened to your ball after you hit your drive. Is it in the water, on the roof of the Duomo, or perchance even on the fairway? You'll be so busy maintaining your footing on the narrow outreach tee box that you won't have a clue! The difficulty in making this drive, of course, stems from the fact that the tower is approximately 16 feet off the perpendicular.

When Bonnano Pisano, the course architect, designed his signature hole, he created a stunningly unique and enormously difficult par 4. Assuming a successful launch from the tower, one still has the unenviable task of holding the green with a wood or long iron from 220-plus yards out. As if that weren't enough, bunkers flank the entire green with "bogey" written all over them. A par here is well earned indeed.

4th
HOLE
PAR 3
165 YARDS

The heavily bunkered par-3 4th hole.
Many players choose to play the 4th
long and carom off the Duomo.

Photo: Mauritius/Superstock

Another lovely and challenging hole at the Tower is the par-4, dog-leg right, 447-yard 8th hole. You'll need a strong approach shot to clear the camposanto (cemetery) that is located on the north side of the piazza and which, incidentally, is said to contain earth from the Holy Land. If you find yourself in one of the many bunkers that border the green, be forewarned that the sand here is often deceptively light. Swing that wedge al dente!

The 17th is a tricky par-3, 174-yard hole that plays directly over the Baptistry to an elevated, floating green in the center of the Piazza del Duomo. (The old course played entirely on land—Arnold Palmer added the water and novel floating green along with his other course renovations in the late 1970s.) Use the small locator flag on the top of the Baptistry to orient your shot to the green. If you're on your game, you'll enjoy one of the most serene moments the game of golf has to offer, as you are taken by gondola to your waiting putt.

GOLF COURSES YOU'LL NEVER PLAY

Designed by Bonnano Pisano in 1173, course improvements by Arnold Palmer in 1976, 6,745 yards, par 72. Be sure to visit the Duomo pro shop—surely one of the largest and best-stocked pro shops in the world. If you're on a tight schedule, request one of the special Alfa Romeo carts that can be seen driving the course at top speeds of 120 kilometers per hour!

The spectacular Leaning Tower and the Duomo border the 16th at the Tower. (The tower itself has been closed since 1902—except to golfers, of course.)

Photo: Benn Mitchell/The Image Bank

The Taj Mahal
Mausoleum, Golf & Country Club
Agra, India

As YOU ENTER the 100-foot-high, three-story arched entranceway to the main gate of the Taj Mahal Mausoleum, Golf & Country Club, you can't help but notice that this is not just another country club. Far from it.

Designed for Shah Jahan, this course (and mausoleum) took 20,000 men and women, laboring day and night, some 22 years to complete. Once it was finished, the emperor was so pleased with the results that he chopped off the hands of the master builders—insuring that they would never build another course as spectacular as the Taj. In surveying the other courses of the region, it would seem the emperor's wish was granted!

The Taj Mahal clubhouse (and mausoleum) forms a dramatic backdrop for the 415-yard, par-4 7th hole.

Photo: Prim and Ray Manley/Superstock

When speaking of the Taj, it is of course the signature 18th that first comes to mind. Here is the hole that beckons linksters from around the world to come and test the limits of their game. At 344 yards, it is a difficult par 3. When you consider that all but three of these yards are over water, you quickly come to appreciate the true meaning of the term "water hazard." (This body of water has likely caught more poorly hit golf balls than any other hazard in the world. If you look closely, you can spot golf balls dating back over 200 years!) As you approach the green, keep

a sharp eye out for the cow pies—they're absolutely everywhere!

While the 12th is the cornerstone of this 300-year-old course, it is far from the only hole of note. The 275-yard, par-3 4th is a breathtaking hole—literally. The tee box is situated at 138 feet straight up in the northeast minaret. The hole plays straight and mostly down, over several cypresses. Be sure to test the winds prior to making your shot.

The dog-leg left 9th is one of the trickier par-4 holes you'll encounter. This hole is bordered by the muddy Agra River (little more than a stream) and the Ja-wab, a large structure that sits directly behind the Taj clubhouse and mausoleum. Unforgiving tile work surrounds the entire fairway and green. Pinpoint accuracy on the 4th is a must, so now is as good a time as any to cash in on any good karma you've accrued in this life.

Designed for Shah Jahan in 1631; 5,692 yards, par 69. Turbans suggested year-round. Caddies required. Be sure to visit the five-star Top O' the Taj— India's only revolving restaurant and mausoleum. Nehru jackets required.

LEFT: *A Taj marshal presides over opening day.*

Photo: Lisl Dennis/The Image Bank

RIGHT: *Balls that stray from the fairway are difficult to play off the tiles on the 9th. In the background is the Ja-wab, where you can grab a quick hot dog or Coke as you head for the back nine.*

Photo: G. K. and Vikki Hart/The Image Bank

The New York Stock Exchange & Country Club
Wall Street
New York City, New York
United States

THE WORLD'S ONLY 18-HOLE **indoor golf course** is also the site of the world's largest stock exchange. In fact, The New York Stock Exchange & Country Club is the only place where you can lose big money on and off the course at the same time!

Focus and concentration are the keys to mastering the Exchange. With traders yelling out their buy-and-sell orders at the top of their lungs, even the most composed golfer can lose his or her cool. (Regular players report that it is not uncommon, while putting out, to be knocked over by a frenzied trader.)

The course at the Exchange is littered with old order tickets, and the artificial lighting makes reading the greens all but impossible. But for those who look upon all of this noise and bustle as a challenge, playing here is a richly satisfying experience.

The Exchange plays on the short side at 1,929 yards. The front nine winds around the trading floor, while the back nine is played on elevated tees and greens suspended above the trading floor. At 187 yards, the first hole is a challenging dog-leg left, dog-leg right, then dog-leg left again, par 3. The fairway is exceedingly narrow, so do not become alarmed if you mishit; included in your greens fees is full indemnification from any injury you may cause to

As you wait to putt out on the 3rd, check your putts on monitors within easy view.

Photo: Al Satterwhite/The Image Bank

traders on the floor. Everyone on the Exchange floor trades *at their own risk!*

The front nine concludes with a delightful 122-yard par 3 that plays directly over a particularly

10th Hole
PAR 3
118 YARDS

Before teeing off at the short 10th hole, you may want to check your
short positions on the video monitors directly above the ball washer.

frenzied trading kiosk and in front of the upstairs gallery. Making the green here is critical, since the bunkers surrounding the green tend to attract empty Coke cans, cigar and cigarette butts, fast-food leftovers, and twisted Rolaids wrappers.

The back nine at the Exchange is really a misnomer— top nine is more like it. From each of these holes you'll have a spectacular view of the action on the course and trading floor below. Indeed, it is here that you may also run into one of the course's most infamous golfers— Ivan Boesky. (While his floor privileges were revoked and his assets seized in 1985, Boesky still retains his membership in the Stock Exchange Club.)

While playing the top nine, you're no longer on the floor per se, but this doesn't mean you can't still keep on eye on your investments. Monitors with up-to-the-second trading data are always within view. In fact, wherever you look, there seem to be monitors at the New York Stock Exchange & Country Club— insuring you a wonderful day of golf *and* financial speculation.

Designed by Robert Trent Jones, Jr.; 1,929 yards, par 51. Opening bell signals start of play and trading each morning at 9:30 A.M., eastern standard time. Members only. (Limited membership is available in the high six-figure range and includes trading privileges at no additional charge.)

Up-to-the-minute golf scores and stock prices scroll by at the only PGA-sanctioned indoor golf course in the world.

Photo: Bob Greisen

The Great Pyramids
Giza, Egypt

WHEN KING KHUFU DESIGNED the Great Pyramids golf course (along with his final resting place), he wasn't concerned with expense or time. The pharaoh had a notoriously poor swing, and even with his five wood, he was rarely able to get the ball elevated off the tee box. Khufu was after a course that would make his game look good—and that's exactly what he created with the massively elevated tees you'll find at the Great Pyramids.

When the Great Pyramids first opened nearly 4,500 years ago, only the pharaoh was permitted to tee off from the championship tees located at the very top of the six course pyramids. Today, anyone can have the pleasure of watching his or her drive hit from atop one of these large stone edifices soar out into the clear blue desert sky.

The 10th was Khufu's favorite hole. (He liked this hole so much that upon his death he was entombed below the championship tees at the 10th.) At 675 yards, it's a long dog-leg left par 5—but no need to worry, as the 482-foot elevated tee will help you get the job done. Endless bunkers border the entire length of the narrow fairway. Another bunker—or is it the same one?—surrounds the green.

A caddy makes a club selection on the third hole. In the distance, just barely visible, a golfer tees off from one of the six elevated tees at Pyramids.

Photo: Butch Martin/The Image Bank

The 14th at Pyramids is perhaps the most celebrated golf hole in the world. In what surely provided the inspiration for Pete Dye's 17th hole at TPC at the Sawgrass

To add some variety to the many bunkers at this course, some traps have been riddled with jagged-edged rocks.

Photo: Guido Alberto Ross/The Image Bank

course, you'll drive to an island green located in an old, now flooded, limestone quarry. This 387-yard, par-4 hole also boasts more than its fair share of bunkers. A large sphinx (designed with the body of a lion and the head of a golfer) sits dead center in the fairway at the 150-yard marker—providing one of the most daunting psychological and physical obstacles you're likely to encounter in the game.

Pyramids is a remarkable course. When one considers that this 18-hole PGA championship course was built by hand without the use of any heavy earth-moving equipment at all, one comes to appreciate its unique place in the history of the game. How did the ancient Egyptians move all of that topsoil to this desert site? How were the fairways kept green, day in and day out, under the scorching desert sun? And how did they know about Bermuda grass—thousands of years before the colony of Bermuda even existed? The answers to these questions will remain eternally buried, along with the mummified remains of King Khufu.

Designed by King Khufu, fourth Dynasty, in 2680 B.C.; 6,452 yards (from the championship tees), par 72. Pyramids is a short drive from Cairo. Dress appropriately; temperatures can reach 150 degrees in the summer!

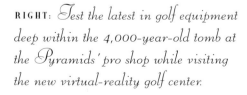

ABOVE: *Don't leave your sand wedge at home if you intend to conquer the Great Pyramids!*

Photo: Derek Berwin/The Image Bank

RIGHT: *Test the latest in golf equipment deep within the 4,000-year-old tomb at the Pyramids' pro shop while visiting the new virtual-reality golf center.*

Photo: Ronald R. Johnson/The Image Bank

GOLF COURSES YOU'LL NEVER PLAY

The Ruins
Stonehenge Golf & Country Club
Salisbury Plain, England

For many years it was believed that the big stones of Stonehenge were the remains of some type of religious temple or an early type of astronomical observatory, a giant calendar of the seasons. In recent years, though, the precise nature of this structure has finally been revealed: it is the remains of what was surely the world's oldest clubhouse of the world's oldest golf course.

For some time, archaeologists mistakenly believed that Stonehenge was built as an enormous calendar. This erroneous assumption was made because on the longest day of the year, June 21, the sun rises directly over the top of one of the big rocks that supported the original roof to the clubhouse. What these early archaeologists failed to take into

account, though, was the significance of this date to golfers around the world. Being the longest day of the year, June 21 affords golfers enough time to play a full round of golf even after putting in a full day at the office. Clearly, the Stonehenge clubhouse and course was designed to celebrate this best of all golfing days.

Today, Stonehenge has been

The 9th hole, affectionately known as "Fish 'n' Chips," is a long 735-yard par 5. Be certain not to overhit your approach to the green—you may lose your ball for an eternity.

Photo: Pete Turner/The Image Bank

brought back to its original splendor under the caring eye of Robert Trent Jones, Jr. As you prepare to tee off high above the

course, standing atop the first monolithic rock, you can't help but appreciate the grandeur of the ruins. Here is a course that is rough and long—real long, at over 10,000 yards. There are no fairways per se. In fact, the entire course is little more than a vast, open clearing. But don't be misled by these wide-open fairways. Stonehenge is an enormously

challenging course. Well-bunkered greens are nestled in among the rocks, and a total of 7 of the 18 holes play back to this, the original clubhouse location. An approach shot here must be made with scientific precision or the results can be disastrous. Cows roam much of the course too, and serve as unpredictable moving hazards to the unsuspecting golfer.

In all, Jones has managed to create a first-class golf resort destination while maintaining the integrity of the original course design. (In fact, not one of the monolithic stones was moved from its original location.)

Little is known about the Old Course. Sadly, the earliest golfers at Stonehenge had no written language, so they were unable to

leave us any written history of their course and country club. Questions such as "How much were the monthly dues?" and "How were handicaps computed before numbers?" will likely remain unanswered. Thankfully, though, as in years past, linksters can once again enjoy this granddaddy of all courses.

Designed "naturally" from the time of the Celts; approximately 2200 B.C. Old Course played between 10,000 and 20,000 yards, par unknown. New Course, designed by Robert Trent Jones, Jr., in 1990, is 10,007 yards, par 107. Two-hour drive from London.

The signature big rocks and rough natural fairway of the Stonehenge Golf & Country Club. The stone clubhouse was built over 2,000 years before the birth of Christ.

Photo: Harald Sund/The Image Bank

The Vatican City Golf & Country Club
Vatican City
Rome, Italy

FOR MANY OF US, playing golf is a religion: we are faithful in making our weekly tee times; the game gives us a wonderful sense of purpose and belonging; and we do an awful lot of praying while we play. And of all the fine courses you may play around the world, none will bring you closer to a "religious experience" than the Vatican City Golf & Country Club.

The front nine of the Vatican plays in the enclosed square of Saint Peter's. The first nine holes are not particularly difficult at the Vatican—perhaps what poses the greatest threat to your game is being hit by an errant shot from one of the many adjacent open fairways. If you approach these holes with a pure heart, you'll attain par.

The one exception is the par-4, dog-leg left, 397-yard 7th. It's a real doozy. A large Egyptian obelisk sits well into the fairway at 100 yards out at the 7th—and claims more than its fair share of mishit drives. While the green is not difficult to hold with your approach shot, depending upon your lie, you may have a tough time spotting the pin. Ask a local how to line up your shot using the Patron Saint of Lost Causes, whose statue is visible high above the green, as your marker.

Previous winners of the Pontiff Invitational are enshrined on the clubhouse roof overlooking the front nine.

Photo: Clark Weinberg/The Image Bank

While the front nine is a wide-open tract, the back nine is wooded and serene—a true golfer's sanctuary. After passing through Saint Peter's Church, you'll find the tee box for the 10th just to the south. This par-5, 485-yard hole wouldn't pose much of a threat if it weren't for the fact that the championship tees are situated directly behind a set of massive and unforgiving Grecian columns. If you don't hit this drive straight as an arrow, the ricochet may be the Maker's way of sending you straight to "the back nine in the sky."

The 16th is Pope Paul's favorite. Large chestnut trees border the fairway along this lovely 355-yard, par-4 hole. Here as elsewhere on the back nine, in place of traditional water traps you'll find spectacular fountains. In the center of the fairway, right at the 125-yard marker, is a 30-foot-high fountain modeled

after a seventeenth-century galleon, with sixteen water-shooting cannons. (This is course architecture that you will never see again—in this life!) At the approach to the green, three bottomless bunkers protect it and stand ready to tempt your ball from its true and righteous path to the pin.

While the Vatican course is often crowded, and certainly plays on the slow side, a pilgrimage to this fine old course is well worth the time and expense.

_____

Course is 6,586 yards, par 71. Any denomination may play. Closed on Easter and Christmas, but open late on Good Friday. Club members and nonmembers alike must observe the strict dress code. For tee times, please make

A view from above Saint Peter's, looking down on the majestic front nine of the Vatican course.

Photo: Simon Wilkinson/The Image Bank

an application to the Prefettura della Casa Pontifica. After a round of golf, be sure to take in the charming Sistine Chapel with its impressive Michelangelo—situated just east of the clubhouse.

The Presidential Course
The White House
Washington, D.C.
United States

YOU DON'T HAVE TO BE A GOLFER to recognize the significance of this address: 1600 Pennsylvania Avenue. But if you are one, you'll know that this is also the location of the golf course of presidents. This is where the leaders of the world shank their shots, make their bets, and enjoy the camaraderie of the 19th over a few drinks. There is no course in the United States more exclusive than the Presidential Course.

Located in the heart of Washington, D.C., the Presidential Course is not a particularly challenging course in the traditional sense of the word. The true challenge in playing the course of presidents comes not from the golf course layout, but from the fact that the White House is almost always within view and within striking distance. An errant shot on the 3rd, 7th, 9th, 11th, 15th, or 18th can easily shatter one of the hundreds of White House windows that front the course. (Each and every year a bill to install protective netting around the White House is presented, debated, and rejected by Congress.)

On the 99-yard 1st hole, you'll want to bring your pitching wedge. But other than your putter, you won't need to bring any other clubs with you for your entire

A quiet autumn afternoon at the 18th.

Photo: Medford Taylor/Superstock

outing. (At just 18 acres, the course is on the small side.) Take the elevator to the third floor, high above the South Portico. Behind the curved balustrade you'll find the tee-off mat for the first hole. Hit straight and hit short.

The dog-leg left 15th plays directly over the famous Rose

Our 42nd president extricates himself from a fairway bunker.

Garden, which is located just outside the president's office in the West Wing. You'll make the green in two, unless you're aiming for a birdie, which will call for a well-placed shot directly over the West Wing. Good luck!

Every president since John Adams has lived in the White House, and each regularly played the Presidential Course. The only president who did not live here was George Washington; however, the course design is based on sketches George created during the boring parts of the First Congress. And, over the years, the course has changed. Each presi-

dent and his family have left their mark. Teddy Roosevelt increased the overall size and depth of many of the bunkers. LBJ installed the spouting fountains—which reminded him of his oil wells back home—in the water hazard fronting the 9th. During the Ford administration, large overhead mirrors on the 8th, 13th, and 15th were installed. (These

precautionary mirrors were needed after a number of players were inadvertently hit when the president teed off.) And most recently, Nancy Reagan oversaw the design and installation of the "Presidential Ball Washers" at each of the women's tee boxes. As our country changes, so changes the Presidential Course.

Originally designed by our country's first president, George Washington. New course by Robert Trent Jones after World War II; 3,043 yards, par 71. Course is closed during outdoor press conferences, award ceremonies, and high-level diplomatic meetings. Call the White House and press 12, former vice-president Dan Quayle's old extension, for tee times.

As you approach the 9th, fountains play in the majestic South Lawn water hazard. The well-stocked pro shop is located under the South Portico.

Photo: Robert Kristofik/The Image Bank